How to Write a Business Plan

Step by Step guide

Entrepreneur Series

Manuel Taylor

Mendon Cottage Books

JD-Biz Publishing

Disclaimer

The information is this book is provided for informational purposes only. It is not intended to be used and medical advice or a substitute for proper medical treatment by a qualified health care provider. The information is believed to be accurate as presented based on research by the author.

The contents have not been evaluated by the U.S. Food and Drug Administration or any other Government or Health Organization and the contents in this book are not to be used to treat cure or prevent disease.

The author or publisher is not responsible for the use or safety of any diet, procedure, or treatment mentioned in this book. The author or publisher is not responsible for errors or omissions that may exist.

Warning

The Book is for informational purposes only and before taking on any diet, treatment, or medical procedure, it is recommended to consult with your primary health care provider.

Our books are available at
1. Amazon.com
2. Barnes and Noble
3. Itunes
4. Kobo
5. Smashwords
6. Google Play Books

Table of Contents

Introduction

If you have bought this short book, you are probably thinking about starting your own business. We live in the 21st century and we have more business opportunities now than ever before. Today, it is possible to start a global online business and to manage companies that are thousands of miles away from home. The technology has made our lives much easier.

The reason you are reading this book is probably not because you don't have the idea, but because you need to create a business plan and convince investors that what you plan to do is profitable. Before you continue reading this book, I want to tell you that there is nothing to be afraid of. Yes, writing a business plan is a bit difficult and complicated, as you need to pay attention to details, but yes, you can write it!

In this short guide, we will go step by step through everything you need to know in order to write a business plan. Also, I am going to create a fictitious company and create a business plan for it. That way you can see how a complete business plan is written step by step.

Before we start, you need to know that when you are writing the business plan, you should not only think as yourself, but as the owner, as well. Remember, the goal is not to convince you. The goal is to convince the investors. So you need to put yourself in the position of the investor and make sure that what you have written is done really, really well.

The key to writing a good business plan is not only to have all the sections written such as Marketing plan, financial projection, and so on, but also to have answered all the questions that the investor might have for the project you're presenting. Always keep this in mind. I will remind you of this many times during this book as I am going to write the potential questions with *italic font*.

This was a short introduction to what to expect in this book. Now, let's get started!

Structure of the business plan

There is no right or wrong structure. There is no structure that everyone uses. As mentioned in the introduction, your goal is to answer all the questions that the investors might have and prove that your idea is profitable. So, as long as you have done that within your business plan, your structure is good. But remember, **what investors want is to see that your business is profitable and it can repay the debt.**

Banks are usually asking for a mortgage, but they don't really want that. Their goal is not to get someone's car or house and then sell it. They don't want to lose time and resources to advertise and find buyers. They don't really care for the mortgage. The mortgage is a sign of how confident the person asking for the loan is in his/her business.

So again, what investors want to see is that your business will generate profit in the future and it can repay the debt.

For the fictitious company that I am going to create through this book, I am going to use the following structure:

- Executive summary

- Company and financing

- Strategic and market analysis

- Marketing plan

- Financial projections

As you might have seen, the executive summary was written last in the table of contents. The reason I recommend you write that part last and then put it at the beginning of your business plan is because it is a summary of your whole business plan. It should be less than a page and should summarize everything that you've written. We'll go through this at the last chapter of this book. Now, let's move on and see what this fictional company will create.

Company and financing

This is a section that seems very important, but is not really, as the investors will not pay it a lot of attention. This is not because it is not important, but because it is not as important as the financial projection section, and the strategic and market analysis section.

In this section, you have to describe your company and the product that your company will manufacture or the service that it will provide to customers.

Now, let's imagine that there's a person named Mr. Smith. He wants to open a burger stand named XYZ and he needs our help to create a business plan. This is the fictitious company, and I am going to create a business plan for XYZ and put all parts together at the end.

In this section, you have to start with describing the company and its employees (if there are any).

Company overview

For our fictitious company, let's say that XYZ was founded by Mr. Smith and it is registered as a sole-proprietorship in the State of California.

Employees

How much money will XYZ spend for salaries?

Do they have experience?

Are you sure that they are the right people you need?

These are the types of questions you can expect in this section. It is highly recommended to write the answers of the potential questions as part of your business plan.

There are 3 employees:

- Jim – He has 4 years' experience working in a fast food restaurant.

- John – He is responsible for the delivery and inventories.

- Jerry – He is 32 years old with 11 years' experience. His last job was at the same fast food restaurant that Jim worked. In fact, they worked together for two years.

The monthly salary will be $3,000 for Jim and Jerry, and $2,800 for John. The total amount of money that XYZ will pay for salaries per year is $105,600.00. This is a fixed cost and it does not depend on the number of hot-dogs and hamburgers that XYZ will sell.

The company will hire two more people if Mr. Smith decides that XYZ will work another shift.

Product/Service

The next part is describing the product that the company will manufacture or the service it will offer.

Why this product?

Why this service?

These are the questions that you can expect to be asked in this section, so make sure you answer them within your business plan. There are two reasons why to manufacture a good or provide a service:

1. There is a problem that is not solved yet and your company, through this service or product, solves it.

2. There is an opportunity to make money and you can use it.

These are the only 2 right answers to the questions listed at the top of this chapter.

Obviously, the burger stand does not solve a problem that has not been solved yet. So, the reason why Mr. Smith wants to open a burger stand is because he saw an opportunity to make money.

Remember, the business plan is always written in 3rd person.

In this section, I need to explain what the burger stand will provide. As the name says, I only need to explain the products/services that the business offers.

In this case, XYZ burger stand will sell a variety of hamburgers and hot-dogs.

However, I haven't described what makes XYZ better than the other similar companies, at least not yet. This is very important in order to get a loan. I am going to write what makes this company better than the competitors in the Strategic and Market analysis.

Financing

This is a very important part. This is where you ask for the amount of money you need for your business.

However, make sure you not only ask for the amount you need for equipment, but also for operating expenses.

Why? Well, if you start with enough money to buy equipment, you won't have any money to buy raw materials. So do your calculation and make sure you ask for the right amount of money. Also, you need to explain why you need the money. You can't just go to an investor and say that you need $100,000.00

Mr. Smith is seeking to raise $60,000.00. The interest rate that XYZ is willing to pay for this loan is 9% fixed interest for a 10-years loan.

The amount of $60,000.00 will be used for:

- $37.000 - Capital to purchase XYZ's equipment

- $22.850 - Financing the first two months of the operations

- $150 - Marketing

Location

The location is very important, especially for a Burger stand. This is something that must be included.

Do you think it is a good location?

XYZ's location is on Street fictitious 1/7 next to the High school MMM.

Another thing you need to have in mind is to be honest. Always be honest!

If you think the location is amazing or it is not good, say it. It is much better if you say it. Remember, you have to answer the potential questions, that way the investors will know that you actually have spent time thinking about your business and you know every part of it.

Strategic and market analysis

How many companies provide the same service?

How many companies manufacture the same product?

How are you going to position yourself?

Why do you think you will survive against them?

This section and the financial projection one are the 2 most important sections in the whole business plan. The investors will pay attention when you reach this part, so you have to be careful. As mentioned in the beginning, **you need to convince the investors that your business is profitable and it can repay the debt.** How do you do that? I created a couple of subsections to make it easier to read.

Industry analysis

The first subsection is the industry analysis. You can find all kinds of statistics on Internet, and you need to know what is relevant for your business plan. All you need to prove in this section is that the industry has the ability to generate profit. This is what I think is relevant for the XYZ business plan:

Number of restaurants in the US – over 650,000

Gross annual receipts in the industry – over $200 billion per year

Employees in this industry – over 10.6 million people

Restaurants that offer similar products/service as XYZ – around 80,000

These 80,000 restaurants generate around 18% of all the revenue generated by restaurants in the United States.

Competition

Remember, the 4th potential question is the most important one. You have to show the investors why your business is better than the others are. You have to find something that makes your business better than the competitors do. You can create a SWOT (strength-weakness-opportunity-threat) analysis or you can just mention everything in a paragraph.

XYZ will face competition mostly from local restaurants. However, we target the students that study in High School MMM as well as the people who live in a radius of 600 meters of the company's location. XYZ will differentiate itself by serving fresh products at cheaper prices than the competitors serve.

XYZ will be opened from 6 a.m. to 2 p.m. As it was mentioned, it is near the high school, so we expect a lot of students as customers as there is only one more place in the neighbor where they can buy fast food.

Pricing

This is the section where you explain the price of your products.

XYZ intends to price its food products between $1.50 and $3.50, depending on the product. The price is also an advantage of XYZ compared to the competition around.

Marketing plan

How are you going to advertise your business?

Is that enough?

How much will it cost?

The marketing plan is always important, regardless of the size of the company that the business plan is for.

Remember the following:

If you have a good product and bad marketing, it will take a long time until your product gets noticed.

If you have a bad product and good marketing, many people will buy your product, but only once.

Make sure you have both!

As for the XYZ fictitious company:

XYZ will use two marketing strategies:

- Use the word-of-mouth marketing by providing quality service to all the customers. This is XYZ's main marketing strategy.

- Implement a campaign via coupons that will provide discounts to the users. These coupons will be given in stores around XYZ and can be used within 48 hours.

Using these two marketing strategies, XYZ is expected to attract enough customers to generate more sales than the break-even point. According to our calculations, XYZ will spend $50 per month for marketing.

(Break-even point will be explained in the next section)

Financial projections

How do you know how much revenue you will generate from sales?

Are you sure your calculations are correct?

If you read everything carefully, you would see that I have written a lot of the costs that XYZ will have. There are still costs that I need to calculate such as tax, depreciation, insurance, rent, utilities, and administrative expenses. First, let's find all of these costs as they are also fixed.

At the beginning, we said that Mr. Smith needs $37,000 to buy equipment. What this means is that the company has a $37,000 / 10 = $3,700 depreciation expense every year.

XYZ has a cost of $1,100 for rent and utilities per month. That's $13,200 per year.

XYZ has a monthly cost of $100 for insurance. Insurance cost per year is $1,200.

XYZ has a monthly cost of $50 to an accounting firm. Administrative costs per year are $600.

XYZ has an interest expense of 9% per year. Interest expense is $5,242.00 for year 1, $4,878.83 for year 2 and $4,480.92 for year 3. You can find loan amortization calculators online to find the interest rate you have to pay.

All of these costs are easy to find and calculate.

All the financial information that we wrote so far is correct. What makes the financial projections hard to do is the other part. The revenue generated. This is something that cannot be known for sure.

For this purpose, I recommend you create 3 different scenarios. The first one is the optimistic one, where your business makes more revenue than you expect. The pessimistic one is where it makes less than you expect and you will need a realistic one, as well.

What you expect is not a number that you create! It has to be based on calculations and facts!

How to estimate sales:

According to surveys, burger stands sell 22 hot-dogs and 27 hamburgers per hour on average.

XYZ will work 8 hours a day, from Monday to Friday. If we multiply the numbers, we get around 45,000 hot-dogs and 55,000 hamburgers.

Now, we mentioned that there is only one place where students could buy something to eat, and that is an advantage to XYZ. Due to the weak competition, this number might get much higher. However, we will stick with these number and we will use them for the realistic scenario.

I am going to create a projected profit and loss statement for 3 years under 3 different scenarios.

First of all, I am going to explain how a profit and loss statement is created and what you need to know in order to create one.

The profit and loss statement shows the difference between the revenue (money earned) and the expenses (costs that the business incurs through that time). If this difference is positive, then the company has net profit, and if it is negative, then the company has net loss.

Now, the weakness of this statement is that it does not say the money you earned is collected! You can have $100,000 revenue and you can profit according to this statement, but maybe you don't have enough money to pay your obligations. So, this is a good statement to show the ability of the company to generate revenue, but it does not show that it actually collected the money.

In our case, it is not that big of a problem, as there are no sales on credit since the business collects the money immediately. However, if you have a big business company and you manufacture a lot of products, you will have to create an additional statement; the cash flow statement. We will take a look at that as well.

As it was mentioned earlier, we need to create 3 scenarios. These scenarios will have different assumptions and these assumptions MUST BE written and said.

Where do we start? We will start with the pessimistic scenario.

Just a reminder, you must have an explanation for every single number that you put on the statement!

How to Create a Profit and Loss Statement

Scenario 1 – Pessimistic

As it was said earlier, you need to start with assumptions.

Assumption 1:

Number of hot-dogs sold in year 1 – 40,000

Number of hamburgers sold in year 1 – 50,000

As you can see, the number of hotdogs and hamburgers sold are reduced by 5,000 each. This is what makes the scenario pessimistic.

In order to calculate the revenue, we multiply the number of sales with its price.

40,000 hotdogs multiplied by $1.5 = $60,000

50,000 hotdogs multiplied by $3.0 = $150,000

Total revenue: $210,000

Assumption 2:

The number of sales will increase by 4% every year.

The equipment will be depreciated over 10 years under the straight-line depreciation method.

We are done with our assumptions. Now we need to create the whole statement. First, let's calculate the operating (gross) profit.

The gross margin is 70%, so 30% of the revenue generated is the cost of goods sold. Our gross profit is 70% of $210,000, and that's $147,000.

Next, we need to remove the other costs in order to get the Earnings before tax. We need to subtract the total expenses that we wrote earlier.

Total expenses are the sum of payroll, marketing, insurance, rent, utilities, administrative expenses, and interest. We already have all the information to calculate the earnings before tax. All of these summed up are $126,362.00

If we subtract them from the gross profit, we get earnings before tax of $20,638.00

If the tax rate is 20%, it means XYZ will pay $4,127.60 and the net profit of the company for Year 1 is $16,510.40

In order to calculate the net margin, divide the net profit with the total revenue from sales. In our case it is $16,510.40/$210,000.00 = 7.86%

The next step is to calculate the same for Year 2 and Year 3.

I recommend using Excel for calculating this statement as it is much easier. This is how scenario 1 would look like in Excel:

Profit and Loss Statement			
	Year 1	Year 2	Year 3
Sales	$210,000.00	$218,400.00	$227,136.00
Costs of goods sold	$ 63,000.00	$ 65,520.00	$ 68,140.80
Gross profit	$147,000.00	$152,880.00	$158,995.20
Gross margin	70%	70%	70%
Payroll	$105,600.00	$105,600.00	$105,600.00
Marketing	$ 600.00	$ 600.00	$ 600.00
Insurance	$ 1,200.00	$ 1,200.00	$ 1,200.00
Rent and Utilities	$ 13,120.00	$ 13,120.00	$ 13,120.00
Administrative expense	$ 600.00	$ 600.00	$ 600.00
Interest	$ 5,242.00	$ 4,878.83	$ 4,480.92
Total expenses	$126,362.00	$125,998.83	$125,600.92
Earnings before tax	$ 20,638.00	$ 26,881.17	$ 33,394.28
Tax	$ 4,127.60	$ 5,376.23	$ 6,678.86
Net profit	$ 16,510.40	$ 21,504.94	$ 26,715.42
Net Margin	7.86%	9.85%	11.76%

Everything that was explained in the previous pages put together looks like this.

In order to make the next scenario, we need different assumptions. We said that the second scenario will be the realistic one.

Scenario 2 - Realistic

Assumption 1:

Number of hot-dogs sold in year 1 – 45.000

Number of hamburgers sold in year 1 – 55.000

As you can see, in this scenario, I used the expected sales according to the survey.

To calculate the revenue, I am going to multiply the expected number of hot-dogs and hamburgers sold with their prices.

45,000 hot-dogs multiplied by $1.5 = \$67,500.00$

55,000 hot-dogs multiplied by $3.0 = \$165,000.00$

Total revenue: $232,500.00

Assumption 2:

The number of sales will increase by 4% every year.

The equipment will be depreciated over 10 years under the straight-line depreciation method.

As you can see, the only part that is changed is the number of sales.

Profit and Loss Statement			
	Year 1	Year 2	Year 3
Sales	$ 232,500.00	$ 241,800.00	$ 251,472.00
Costs of goods sold	$ 69,750.00	$ 72,540.00	$ 75,441.60
Gross profit	$ 162,750.00	$ 169,260.00	$ 176,030.40
Gross margin	70%	70%	70%
Payroll	$ 105,600.00	$ 105,600.00	$ 105,600.00
Marketing	$ 600.00	$ 600.00	$ 600.00
Insurance	$ 1,200.00	$ 1,200.00	$ 1,200.00
Rent and Utilities	$ 13,120.00	$ 13,120.00	$ 13,120.00
Administrative expense	$ 600.00	$ 600.00	$ 600.00
Interest	$ 5,242.00	$ 4,878.83	$ 4,480.92
Total expenses	$ 126,362.00	$ 125,998.83	$ 125,600.92
Earnings before tax	$ 36,388.00	$ 43,261.17	$ 50,429.48
Tax	$ 7,277.60	$ 8,652.23	$ 10,085.90
Net profit	$ 29,110.40	$ 34,608.94	$ 40,343.58
Net Margin	12.52%	14.31%	16.04%

Scenario 3 - Optimistic

Assumption 1:

Number of hot-dogs sold in year 1 – 50,000

Number of hamburgers sold in year 1 – 60,000

In this optimistic scenario, I am using numbers higher than the ones we got based on the survey. This is what makes this scenario an optimistic one. **Make this scenario optimistic, not impossible!**

50,000 hot-dogs multiplied by $1.5 = $75,000.00

60,000 hot-dogs multiplied by $3.0 = $180,000.00

Total revenue: $255,000.00

Assumption 2:

The number of sales will increase by 3% every year. The reason why it is 3% and not 4% is because obviously there is limit when it comes to sales. You cannot expect that the sales will increase forever. When selling this many hot-dogs and hamburgers, it is much better to assume that the sales will increase, but not as much.

The equipment will be depreciated over 10 years under the straight-line depreciation method.

Profit and Loss Statement			
	Year 1	Year 2	Year 3
Sales	$255,000.00	$262,650.00	$270,529.50
Costs of goods sold	$ 76,500.00	$ 78,795.00	$ 81,158.85
Gross profit	$178,500.00	$183,855.00	$189,370.65
Gross margin	70%	70%	70%
Payroll	$105,600.00	$105,600.00	$105,600.00
Marketing	$ 600.00	$ 600.00	$ 600.00
Insurance	$ 1,200.00	$ 1,200.00	$ 1,200.00
Rent and Utilities	$ 13,120.00	$ 13,120.00	$ 13,120.00
Administrative expense	$ 600.00	$ 600.00	$ 600.00
Interest	$ 5,242.00	$ 4,878.83	$ 4,480.92
Total expenses	$126,362.00	$125,998.83	$125,600.92
Earnings before tax	$ 52,138.00	$ 57,856.17	$ 63,769.73
Tax	$ 10,427.60	$ 11,571.23	$ 12,753.95
Net profit	$ 41,710.40	$ 46,284.94	$ 51,015.78
Net Margin	16.36%	17.62%	18.86%

Now we have completed the profit and loss statement for all three scenarios. According to the assumptions we created in the three scenarios, we can expect a profit between $16,510.00 and $41,710.40.

There are a lot of different financial projections that you can create, but the profit and loss statement is one that you can easily create.

Calculating the break-even point is something that you can do without any previous knowledge. The break-even point shows how many products you need to sell in order to have a net profit of 0. Now, calculating the break-even point is very easy if a company is selling one product.

The formula is **Total fixed expenses / (Selling price per product – variable cost per product)**

Example: If a company has fixed expenses of 10,000 (this includes all the expenses between the gross margin and the earnings before tax), and if the selling price is $3.00 per product, with the variable cost per product at $1.00, then the Break-even point is 10,000 /(3-1) = 5,000.

As you can see, the total revenue would be 15,000, the costs of goods sold would be 5,000, and the gross profit would be 10,000. Exactly the same amount of money that the business needs to pay the fixed expenses.

Why is break-even important?

Well, it shows you the minimum amount of products you need to sell in order to NOT lose money. In the example above, if the company sells less than 5,000 products, the company would have net loss. If it sells over 5,000, it would have net profit.

How to calculate the break-even point if the company has more than 1 product:

The part with the fixed expense stays the same; however, I need to calculate a weighted average.

According to the survey, we need 45,000 hot-dogs and 55,000 hamburgers. The break-even formula needs the sales price for 1 product and its variable costs. In order to create the sales price for XYZ, we need to multiply the sales price of each with its participation.

Participation of hot dogs = 45,000/ (45,000+55,000) = 45%

Participation of hamburgers =55,000/ (45,000+55,000) =55%

Selling price = 45% multiplied by 1(the price of hot-dogs) + 55% multiplied by 3(the price of hamburgers)

Selling price for XYZ = $2.1

The last part we need is the variable expense per product. We need to calculate the weighted average again.

Variable cost per product = 45% multiplied by 0.3 (variable cost for hot-dog) + 55% multiplied by 0.9(variable cost for hamburger)

Variable cost per product = $0.63

We could also multiply the 2.1 with 30%, as the gross profit margin is the same for all products. However, if the margin is different for different products, this is the way to calculate it.

Total fixed expenses = $126,362.00

Now we can calculate our break-even point:

Break-even point = 126.362 / (2.1-0.63) =86.590

What this number means?

Now we need to multiply this number with the participation of the two products.

Hot-dogs = 45% multiplied by 86.590 =38683

Hamburgers = 55% multiplied by 86.590 =47277

What this means is basically that the company must sell over 38,683 hot-dogs and 47,277 hamburgers in order to have net profit, otherwise, the company will have net loss.

Executive Summary

As I mentioned before, you need to start your business plan with an Executive summary, however it is highly recommended to write it after you're done with all the other parts of your business plan.

After completing everything else, you understand your business much better and you can write short and clear summary of everything.

The executive summary should not be very long and it only needs to summarize the whole business plan.

You can create a couple of subcategories in the executive summary and make it easy for the person reading it to understand the purpose of the business plan.

XYZ's Executive summary would look like this:

The purpose of this business plan is to raise $60,000.00. Most of this $37,000.00 will be used for buying new equipment for XYZ Burger stand.

XYZ is a sole-proprietorship company and it was founded by Mr. Smith.

Mr. Smith has seen the opportunity to open a Burger stand on street fictitious 1/7 next to the High school.

Organization

The company will have 3 experienced employees that are experts in this area and they will work full-time.

Mission statement

The mission statement is not the most important part of your business plan, but it definitely is something you must have.

The company's mission is to satisfy the customers by providing quality services at reasonable prices.

Sales

XYZ will sell a variety of hot-dogs and hamburgers. XYZ's gross margin is set to 70%.

According to our calculation, we expect XYZ to sell 45,000 hot-dogs and 55,000 hamburgers in the first year totaling of $232,500.00.

Under this realistic scenario, the company will have a profit of $29,110.40 and the net profit margin is 12.52% during Year 1.

Conclusion

As you can see, creating the whole business plan is not very hard; however, you have to pay attention to every single detail. You cannot have a number that you cannot explain. Everything has to be based on calculations and facts, otherwise you will be rejected, and you will not get a loan.

There are a lot of other things that you can add to your business plan, but what was written until now was something that every business plan must have.

You can add different charts and graphs in order to **convince the investors that your business is profitable and it can repay the debt.** Remember, this is your goal. Always have this in mind when you are writing the business plan. Make sure you already have the answers of the potential questions.

Tip: Before you go and discuss the business plan with an investor, ask a friend to take a look at it and discuss it together. Ask your friend to ask everything that he does not understand about your business. It is much better to find out what you are missing before you go to the real interview.

I've put together everything that I explained in the previous pages in a complete business plan.

The whole business plan

XYZ Burger Stand

Business Plan

Table of contents:

Executive summary

Company and financing

Strategic and market analysis

Marketing plan

Financial projections

Executive summary

The purpose of this business plan is to raise $60,000.00. Most of this $37,000.00 will be used for buying new equipment for XYZ Burger stand.

XYZ is a sole-proprietorship company and it was founded by Mr. Smith.

Mr. Smith has seen the opportunity to open a Burger stand on street fictitious 1/7 next to the High school.

Organization

The company has 3 experienced employees that are experts in this area and they will work full-time.

Mission statement

The company's mission is to satisfy the customers by providing quality services at reasonable prices.

Sales

XYZ will sell a variety of hot-dogs and hamburgers. XYZ's gross margin is set to 70%.

According to our calculations, we expect XYZ to sell 45,000 hot-dogs and 55,000 hamburgers in the first year totaling of $232,500.00. Under this realistic scenario, the company will have a profit of $29,110.40 and the net profit margin is 12.52% during Year 1.

Company and financing

Company overview

XYZ was founded by Mr. Smith and it is registered as a sole-proprietorship in the State of California.

Employees

XYZ has 3 employees:

- Jim – He has 4 years' experience working in a fast food restaurant.

- John – He is responsible for the delivery and inventories.

- Jerry – He is 32 years old with 11 years' experience. His last job was at the same fast food restaurant that Jim worked. In fact, they worked together for two years.

The monthly salary will be $3.000 for Jim and Jerry, and $2.800 for John.

Products/services

XYZ burger stand will sell a variety of hamburgers and hot-dogs.

Financing

Mr. Smith is seeking to raise $60,000.00. The interest rate that XYZ is willing to pay for this loan is 9% fixed for a 10-years loan.

The amount of $60,000.00 will be used for:

- $37.000 - Capital to purchase XYZ's equipment

- $22.850 - Financing the first two months of the operations

- $150 - Marketing

Location

XYZ's location is on street fictitious 1/7 next to the High school MMM. The location is amazing, as there is only one other restaurant around as a direct competitor. There are over 600 students that study in the school and they are potential customers. There are also 7 huge buildings in a radius of 600 meters and there are at least 1.000 people living in that area.

Strategic and Market analysis

Industry analysis

Number of restaurants in the US – over 650,000

Gross annual receipts – over $200 billion per year

Employees in this industry – over 10.6 million people

Restaurants that offer similar products/service as XYZ – around 80,000

These 80,000 restaurants generate around 18% of all the revenue generated by restaurants in the United States.

Competition

XYZ will face competition mostly from local restaurants. However, we target the students that study in High School MMM as well as the people who live in radius of 600 meters of the company's location. XYZ will differentiate itself by serving fresh products at cheaper prices than the competitors serve.

XYZ will be opened from 6 a.m. to 2 p.m. As it was mentioned, it is near the high school so we expect a lot of students as customers as there is only one more place in the neighbor where they can buy food.

Pricing

The company intends to price its food products between $1.50 and $3.50, depending on the product. The price is also an advantage of XYZ compared to the competition around.

Marketing Plan

XYZ will use two marketing strategies:

- Use the word-of-mouth marketing by providing quality service to all the customers. This is XYZ's main marketing strategy.

- Implement a campaign via coupons that will provide discounts to the users. These coupons will be given in stores around XYZ and can be used within 48 hours.

Using these two marketing strategies, XYZ is expected to attract enough customers to generate more sales than the break-even point. According to our calculations, XYZ will spend $50 per month for marketing.

Financial Projections

According to a survey, a burger stand, similar to XYZ, sells 22 hot-dogs and 27 hamburgers per hour on average.

If the numbers are the same for XYZ, it is expected to sell around 45,000 hot-dogs and 55,000 hamburgers by working 8 hours every day, from Monday to Friday.

XYZ has a gross margin of 70%. In order to break-even, the company needs to sell products and generate at least $181,839.00. This revenue can be generated by selling 38,683 hot-dogs and 47,277 hamburgers.

XYZ's annual fixed costs:

- Payroll - $105,600.00

- Marketing - $600.00

- Insurance - $1,200.00

- Rent and Utilities - $13,120.00

- Administrative expense (bookkeeping) - $600.00

- Interest - $5,242.00 (Year 1), 4,878.83 (Year 2), and $4,480.00 (Year 3) - Under the assumption of a 10-years loan of $60,000 with an interest rate of 9%.

In this business plan, there are 3 different scenarios:

- Pessimistic

- Realistic

- Optimistic

There is a profit and loss statement created for each of them.

Scenario 1 – Pessimistic

Assumption 1:

XYZ will sell 40,000 hot-dogs and 50,000 hamburgers in year 1.

Assumption 2:

The number of sales will increase by 4% in year 2 and 4% in year 3.

The equipment will be depreciated over 10 years under straight-line depreciation method.

The tax rate is 20%

Profit and Loss Statement			
	Year 1	Year 2	Year 3
Sales	$210,000.00	$218,400.00	$227,136.00
Costs of goods sold	$ 63,000.00	$ 65,520.00	$ 68,140.80
Gross profit	$147,000.00	$152,880.00	$158,995.20
Gross margin	70%	70%	70%
Payroll	$105,600.00	$105,600.00	$105,600.00
Marketing	$ 600.00	$ 600.00	$ 600.00
Insurance	$ 1,200.00	$ 1,200.00	$ 1,200.00
Rent and Utilities	$ 13,120.00	$ 13,120.00	$ 13,120.00
Administrative expense	$ 600.00	$ 600.00	$ 600.00
Interest	$ 5,242.00	$ 4,878.83	$ 4,480.92
Total expenses	$126,362.00	$125,998.83	$125,600.92
Earnings before tax	$ 20,638.00	$ 26,881.17	$ 33,394.28
Tax	$ 4,127.60	$ 5,376.23	$ 6,678.86
Net profit	$ 16,510.40	$ 21,504.94	$ 26,715.42
Net Margin	7.86%	9.85%	11.76%

In the pessimistic scenario, XYZ has a net profit of $16,510.40 and net margin of 7.86%.

Scenario 2 – Realistic

Assumption 1:

XYZ will sell 45,000 hot-dogs and 55,000 hamburgers in year 1.

Assumption 2:

The number of sales will increase by 4% in year 2 and 4% in year 3.

The equipment will be depreciated over 10 years under straight-line depreciation method.

The tax rate is 20%

Profit and Loss Statement			
	Year 1	Year 2	Year 3
Sales	$232,500.00	$241,800.00	$251,472.00
Costs of goods sold	$ 69,750.00	$ 72,540.00	$ 75,441.60
Gross profit	$162,750.00	$169,260.00	$176,030.40
Gross margin	70%	70%	70%
Payroll	$105,600.00	$105,600.00	$105,600.00
Marketing	$ 600.00	$ 600.00	$ 600.00
Insurance	$ 1,200.00	$ 1,200.00	$ 1,200.00
Rent and Utilities	$ 13,120.00	$ 13,120.00	$ 13,120.00
Administrative expense	$ 600.00	$ 600.00	$ 600.00
Interest	$ 5,242.00	$ 4,878.83	$ 4,480.92
Total expenses	$126,362.00	$125,998.83	$125,600.92
Earnings before tax	$ 36,388.00	$ 43,261.17	$ 50,429.48
Tax	$ 7,277.60	$ 8,652.23	$ 10,085.90
Net profit	$ 29,110.40	$ 34,608.94	$ 40,343.58
Net Margin	12.52%	14.31%	16.04%

Under scenario 2, XYZ will have a profit of $29,110.40 and a net margin of 12.52% in year 1.

Scenario 3 – Optimistic

Assumption 1:

XYZ will sell 50,000 hot-dogs and 60,000 hamburgers in year 1.

Assumption 2:

The number of sales will increase by 3% in year 2 and 3% in year 3.

The equipment will be depreciated over 10 years under straight-line depreciation method.

Profit and Loss Statement			
	Year 1	Year 2	Year 3
Sales	$255,000.00	$262,650.00	$270,529.50
Costs of goods sold	$ 76,500.00	$ 78,795.00	$ 81,158.85
Gross profit	$178,500.00	$183,855.00	$189,370.65
Gross margin	70%	70%	70%
Payroll	$105,600.00	$105,600.00	$105,600.00
Marketing	$ 600.00	$ 600.00	$ 600.00
Insurance	$ 1,200.00	$ 1,200.00	$ 1,200.00
Rent and Utilities	$ 13,120.00	$ 13,120.00	$ 13,120.00
Administrative expense	$ 600.00	$ 600.00	$ 600.00
Interest	$ 5,242.00	$ 4,878.83	$ 4,480.92
Total expenses	$126,362.00	$125,998.83	$125,600.92
Earnings before tax	$ 52,138.00	$ 57,856.17	$ 63,769.73
Tax	$ 10,427.60	$ 11,571.23	$ 12,753.95
Net profit	$ 41,710.40	$ 46,284.94	$ 51,015.78
Net Margin	16.36%	17.62%	18.86%

Under scenario 3, XYZ will have a profit of $41,710.40 and a net margin of 16.36% in year 1.

Author Bio

Manuel Taylor was born in a small town in south Macedonia. He spent the first 18 years of his life in his hometown. After finishing high school, he moved to the capital city and studied Accounting & Auditing for the next 4 years.

After finishing college, he went back in his hometown and spent the next 3 years working in one of the best companies there as an accountant.

He met his wife and now they have 2 children.

Manuel left the company and started working with students where he was teaching the basics of economics, finance, and accounting. He also spent a lot of time working as freelancer on different projects in his city.

Manuel is a respected accountant and a person with expertise in this area. Apart from teaching, he is writing business plans.

Today, he has his own consulting company with 6 employees.

Check out some of the other JD-Biz Publishing books

Gardening Series on Amazon

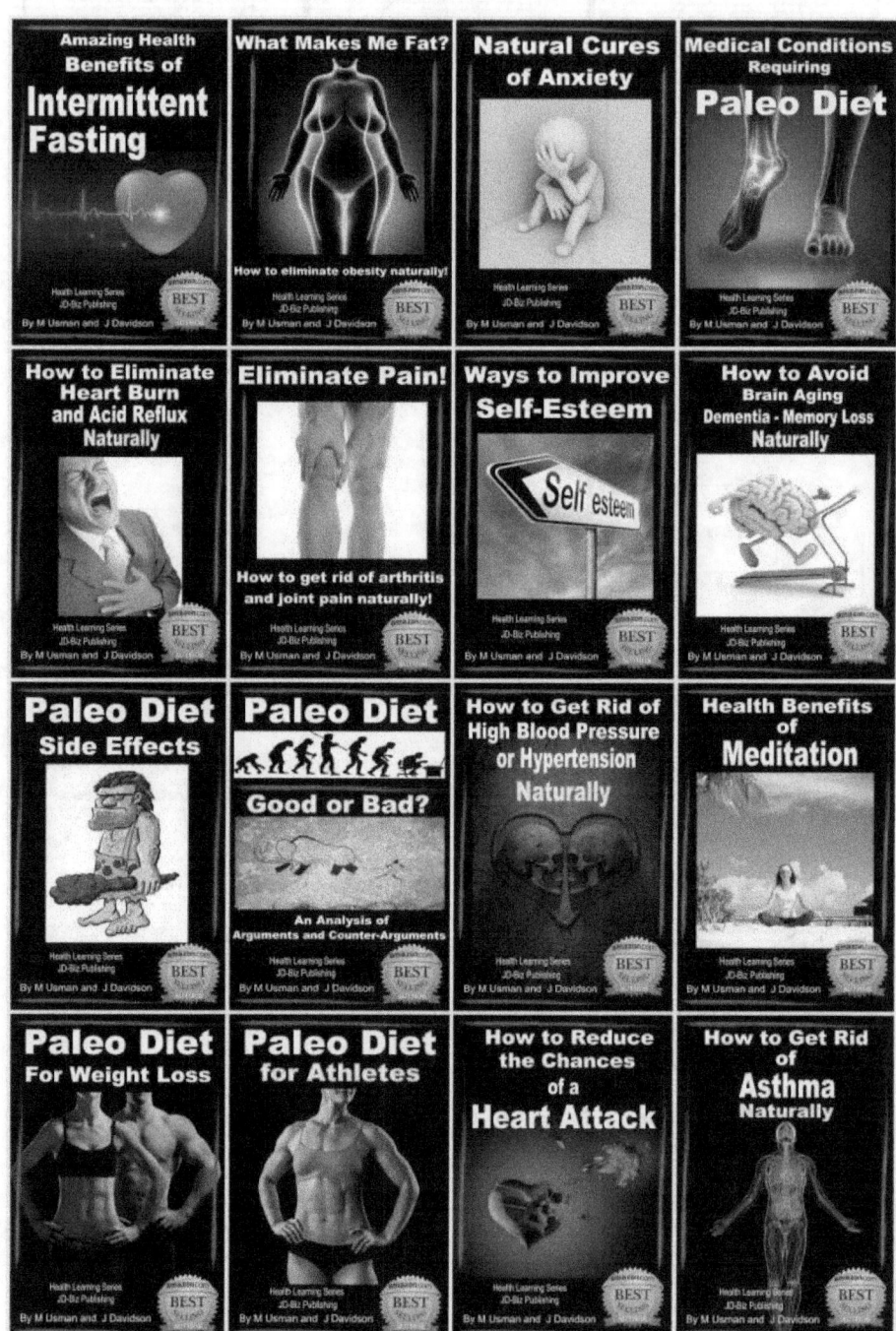

Amazing Animal Book Series

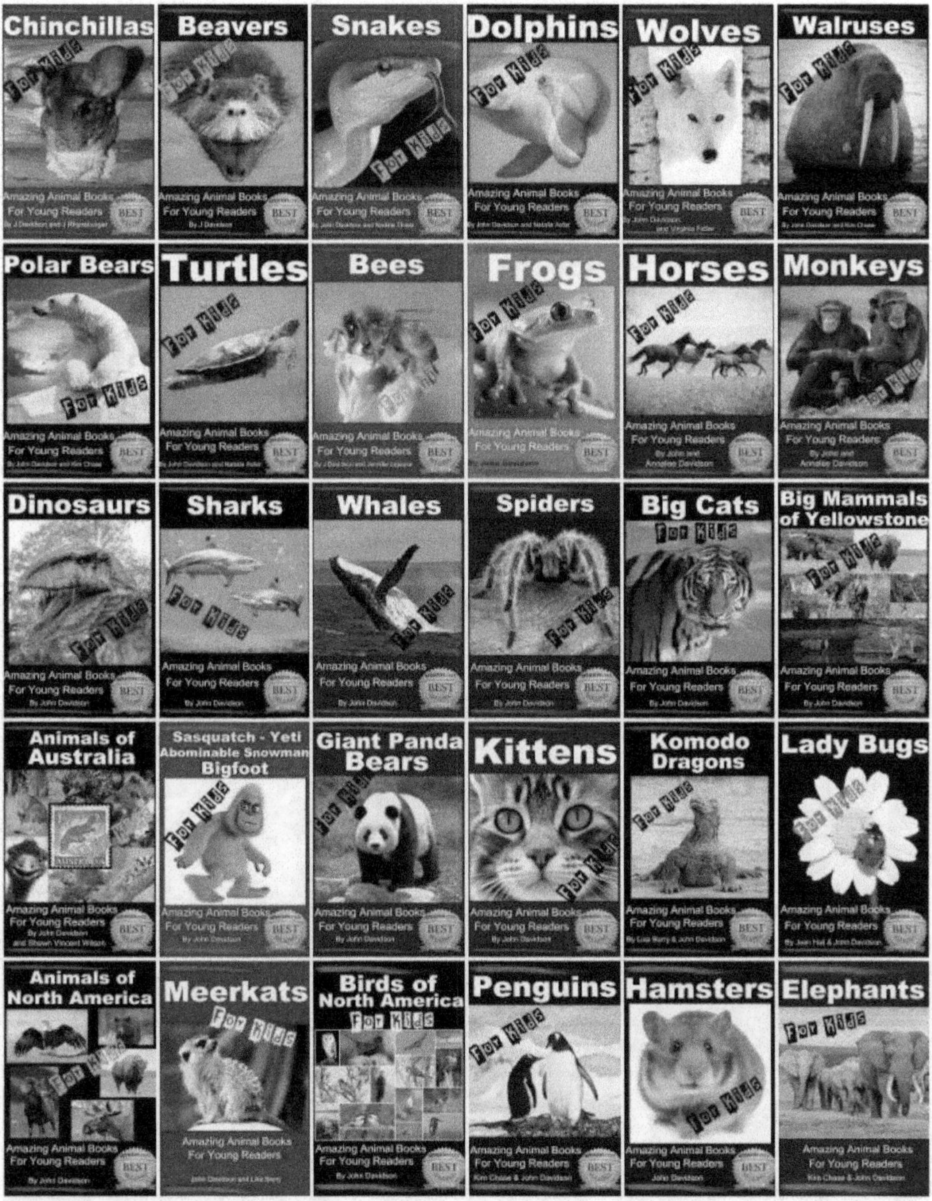

Learn To Draw Series

How to Build and Plan Books

Entrepreneur Book Series

Our books are available at

1. Amazon.com

2. Barnes and Noble

3. Itunes

4. Kobo

5. Smashwords

6. Google Play Books

Publisher

JD-Biz Corp

P O Box 374

Mendon, Utah 84325

http://www.jd-biz.com/

Mendon Cottage Books

P O Box 374, Mendon Utah 84325

www.ingramcontent.com/pod-product-compliance
Lightning Source LLC
Chambersburg PA
CBHW071009180526
45168CB00003B/1348